I've Come Too Far

31 Days of Motivational Affirmations

Derrick Jaxn

Printed in the United States of America

First Printing, 2017
ISBN: 978-0-9910336-5-2
Shop Derrick Jaxn LLC

www.shopderrickjaxn.com

contactshopderrickjaxn@gmail.com

TABLE OF CONTENTS

A s a teenager, I would get caught talking to myself. My friends would see it and laugh. My girlfriend would be puzzled, and I believe deep down, my parents were a little worried although they tried to laugh it off too. I can see why. From the outside, people wouldn't understand, but with the constant flow of messages in, out, and swirling around my head, a few of those conversations were bound to be overheard.

Fast-forward ten years, and that self-talk changed my life. Not because I did it, because many of us do, but because mine was constructive, positive, honest, and motivational. I didn't allow my voice to take on any energy it wanted. I controlled it to intentionally guide me into my destiny.

Some people talk themselves out of opportunities. I talked myself into several. Many talk themselves out of trying, but I talked myself into never giving up. Many people talk themselves into depression. I talked and acted on that talk until I was out of it. While as a teenager, I may have not understood the power of the tongue, but as an adult, there's no denying it. I wouldn't have my family, financial stability, health, or sanity without it.

This book contains the very same messages I've imprinted on my subconscious over the years. The same words that I found strength in when weakness overwhelmed me will now be available to you. No matter if you're striving to be the next billionaire, obtain a Ph.D., or simply live to fight another day, it's my sincere belief that these words will help you do all of the above.

While this book is short and can be consumed in a matter of minutes, do understand that this is a marathon, not a sprint. If you must read through to familiarize yourself with the passages, that's fine. But revisit these chapters regularly so that you can give your mind the vitamins it needs to combat life's ills that will surely come your way if not already knocking at your door. Read through them several times a day, and watch your energy shift one week at a time. Watch the inflow of positive things into your life. Watch your perspective change and enjoy the newfound power over your situation, no matter how bad it may seem. If done correctly, these passages can change the course of your life the same way it did mine. Enjoy.

I've come too far to quit.

I could give up, but I refuse to. I know it would be easier. I'm sure it would be less stressful and emotionally taxing. I'm sure there would be less tears involved and people wanting explanations for why I've "changed" when really, I'm just focused. I'm sure I wouldn't miss out on so much fun and I could watch more TV and sacrifice less time doing the trivial things my peers are doing. I'm willing to bet I'd feel a little better putting money into going out instead of investing in myself with a risk of losing every penny. I have no doubt that calling it quits right now would be less difficult than continuing on with no guarantee that it will all add up to anything at all. But I wasn't designed to be this strong just so I can look for an easy way out. People have sacrificed for me to have the opportunity that's in front of me. I sacrificed to have this opportunity. Therefore, I refuse to just lie down to circumstances I'm faced with. It will have to beat me. Surrendering is not an option. I began this because it was worth it, and I will finish this because I deserve it.

CHAPTER 2

My pain will push me.

Yes, it hurts. Yes, I want to cry sometimes. But if I must cry, I will cry as I push forward. The tears will run down my face, but I will not run and hide from the difficulty I'm experiencing. I will go until there's nothing left and then I will dig deeper and find more so I can fight harder. I will let my pain serve as future memories of the price I paid to make it through my trials, not as my breaking point. Even if I don't feel like I can handle it, I will force myself to go until I physically can not move another inch towards my goals. As long as I have breath in my body, I can and will keep moving, no matter how much it hurts too. I am a winner, and that's what winners do!

CHAPTER 3

My breaking point is only my restart button.

Whatever this is that came to break me chose the wrong one. I don't care who, what, or how many have come against me, if it breaks me, it's only restarting the new me to come back better. I don't break, I rebuild. Stronger. More resilient. Hungrier. More focused. Everything refreshes the moment I hit my knees because I am a fighter, and surrender does not run in my blood. So I may not see a way out. But if I don't, I will make a way out. Nothing will stand in the face of my consistency and desire to go forward. My stumble is not to be mistaken for me stopping, I'm simply catching my breath to get up and go again. I am unbeatable because I am unstoppable. I will not break the promise to myself to try again and again until I am done.

CHAPTER 4

I'm here for a reason.

My disgust with losing is not a mistake. The vision I had when I started was not an accident. Everything I feel when I fall short is by design to keep me going because I am supposed to be here and my work is significant. It will mean more to more people than I could have ever imagined. The day breath filled my lungs, so did purpose fill my heart, and the breath that remains is evidence that so does my purpose. One day, my work will be done, but that day is not today. I am important and so are the lives I'm here to impact.

CHAPTER 5

Folding is not an option.

Although my body says no, my mind says stop, my obstacles say quit, my resources say I can't, my doubters say I won't, my heart has the final say and it says, "Watch me as I do." Against all odds, the ropes, and the devil himself, I'm fully equipped to keep pressing forward. I will not fold. I will expand myself until I've risen to the occasion at hand, and I will conquer.

CHAPTER 6

I'm smarter this time.

It caught me slipping. I wasn't prepared, and I was naive. Those days are gone. I'm better because I know how to defend myself next time. I'm stronger because I've gone through it before and I'm still here. I'm a much-improved version of myself, and because of that, my odds of winning this time are exponentially higher. Once I survive the process it takes to heal from the last hit, I will be much harder to hit. I will see it coming and other attacks like it. There are levels to this, and I'm on a higher one because of it. Everybody gets knocked down sometimes, but not everyone gets back up. But I will because I'm wiser than before. I'll be ready next time.

CHAPTER 7

My prayers are being heard.

Although it feels like my cries for direction and help are stopping at the ceiling, I know my prayers are being heard. I know that God walks with the imperfect, but he will not walk for us. Therefore, I must keep doing my part. I must let this process teach me what it is intended to teach me, and I will learn from it the lessons that will make my journey easier later down the road. But for the time being, I must learn to endure, be patient, and stay focused. I am in the midst of a storm, but that doesn't mean that I am forgotten. I will simply continue working to recognize the tools God has already given me that he's waiting for me to use right now. My prayers are indeed being heard, and I accept that the answer doesn't look the way I thought it would or that it hasn't come in the time I'd like. Either way, I will go on in confidence that God is aware of my struggle, and I am not alone.

CHAPTER 8

My only competition is my former self, and I'm winning.

Imay not be as popular as I once was or as financially set as I once was, but now every experience I've had has pushed me closer to my full potential. I am a success waiting to happen because of all the failures that have already happened. My former self didn't know any better, but now that I do, I can only do better. It does not matter what anyone else thinks or expects. I expect the best out of me, and I will fulfill that prophecy. Competing with others against their perceived position is unnecessary when I've been given my own set of directions to get to the position meant for me. In my career, in my relationships, in my physical well-being, and in my finances, my only competition is myself, and although the charts, graphs, or numbers may not show it, I am winning.

CHAPTER 9

I deserve the things I go to sleep and wake up thinking about.

Success is not some pre-determined divine selective. It's something that starts with a thought or a possibility we began to entertain and then eventually can't shake. That's exactly what I have, therefore I can have it just like anyone else. Since I can have it, I've made up my mind I will have it. Nothing is owed to me, I owe it to myself to get exactly what I can't stop thinking about. I won't let myself settle for less even if I don't meet every goal or achieve every milestone in the time I felt like it would happen. I will not stop believing nor working for my desires. I will earn it with consistency and hard work. I deserve it because I have the audacity to believe it belongs to me, and I will have it because I will not stop until it's mine.

CHAPTER 10

My time is not later, nor has it passed, my time is right now!

I reject any notion that I must wait to affect my future. Even if I don't currently have the money necessary to invest or I'm not in the location best suited to officially begin the next step, I can and will do what I can right now. I will learn. I will observe. I will immerse myself in whatever knowledge I can get my hands on and meditate on the ways I will succeed so that success finds me that much easier when the time comes. My time to embark on the journey to the life I've always wanted is right now. I don't care what has happened to me in the past, or what could happen in the future, I will find a way to make progress right now, right here. I will not wait.

CHAPTER 11

Obstacles are real, fear is not.

Money will be tight. Health may be shaky. Mentally, I may be under a lot of pressure and my emotions are all over the place. But I do not have to fear anything because fear is fake. Anything that comes my way will be met with my best, and what happens after that will take care of itself, therefore I do not have to fear. What's to come may set me back, but I do not have to fear, for I can count on my ability to bounce back from anything. Fear is not real, but my heart is. My hustle is. My grind is. My focus is. My fight is. Fear should fear that because I won't accept fear.

CHAPTER 12

Average is for someone else.

Maybe the others have it a little easier. Maybe they can do without it. Maybe they don't dream about it day and night. Maybe they don't feel sick at the thought of not accomplishing it before they die. Maybe they don't have supporters to prove right and doubters to prove wrong. Maybe they didn't come from nothing. Maybe they didn't go without help they thought they would have. Maybe they had helping hands everywhere they turned and never had to figure it out on their own. But as for me, I know this means something far too important to tolerate anything average. Everything from my schedule to the way I carry myself to the things I indulge in and the way I talk must be far above average because what I'm trying to accomplish is above average. I want it more than the average and have it harder than average so that's something the others can keep. Average is for someone else, I refuse to be average.

CHAPTER 13

They counted me out, God counted me in.

My path isn't dictated by outside perception. I don't have to fit in the box of someone else's expectations. No one can create stipulations for my success or the completion of my goals. They already tried. If it was up to them, I would've been done a long time ago. I would've stopped before I started. I would've given up before I even got started if they were to have the last say. I would've doubted myself and been too ashamed to fail. I would allow their laughs to pierce through my determination and their doubts to suffocate my hope. If it was up to them, I would've been satisfied going through my life wondering "What if?" But it is not up to them. It's up to me and God, only. He will keep me, and I will keep going. We are the only authorities and I will not grant "them" power they don't warrant. I am in full control of my destiny, and my results will show that.

CHAPTER 14

I will outwork my doubts until they no longer exist.

When I begin to wonder if I'm really up for this or if I can handle what's been put in front of me, I will work harder. I will grind as I cry, and I will fight some more. I will get up earlier than I did before, I will stay longer than I originally thought I would have to. I will get the most out of every hour I put into my craft and add hours of work onto it if necessary but I will not tolerate my doubts. I will prove to myself that I am ready for whatever steps my way. Even when progress seems stagnant, I will stay committed to the plan, and I will work. I don't need to rely solely on my talent or anybody's silver spoon. I will get it done with my work ethic and consistency until I can tell even myself, "I told you so."

CHAPTER 15

I will survive until I can thrive again.

This isn't easy. This isn't even fair. Matter of fact, it feels impossible. But this time, I will forget what I feel and remember the mission. Feelings change. The mission doesn't. I will remember why I started and I will slowly stand. I will roll over onto my hands, dig my hands in the dirt, push with everything I have until half of my body is off the ground where I got knocked down. I will steady myself just long enough to drag one leg at a time up until I'm erecting myself again. My back will ache on the way up, and some will see me and feel pity because I will be dirty and my clothes no longer look neat, but I will be doing the most important thing, standing. Not impressing. Not pretending. Not hiding. Not running. I will be standing. And once I'm standing again, I will figure out how to walk again. Once I'm walking I will get back to a slow jog like before. I will jog, then sprint, and then fly...but it all starts with standing and surviving right now.

CHAPTER 16

My pain is proof that I'm getting closer.

I've felt pain, and I've felt comfort. The comfort was the feeling of complacency. It was the feeling of distraction, settling, and being uninspired. But the pain was pressure to do more and try harder. I had to give more of myself because it was hurting. My desire was tested, and I had to pass by going through more even though it didn't feel good. Now I trust that pain. I don't look forward to it, but I look forward to what's on the other side. The pain is here, so the victory is near. Of that, I'm sure.

CHAPTER 17

My disappointments will not deter me.

Yes I believed the lies. I counted on those who let me down, multiple times. I hoped for more and got dealt less. I fell for trickery and trusted the untrustworthy. I applied and got rejected, thought I could do it and failed to get it done. I invested and saw no return. I did all of this as I also let myself down with habits that needed to change... but I will not let my disappointments deter me. I will not give my precious focus to the things and people that are trying to break me. I will give it to my goals. I will give it to my objective. I will keep my energy pointed in the direction of my destiny and I will get there no matter what. I won't allow anyone to get in my way, even myself. I will build myself up and propel myself forward. I will surround myself with people who are helping me go in the same direction, not who try to pull me back. I won't be happy with every choice I'm forced to make, but I will feel more satisfaction with the end result than I would be if I had not made it. I will not be sidetracked, set back, or deterred. I will achieve everything I set out to do!

CHAPTER 18

I will see the positive in the impossible.

When my circumstances say no, I will say louder, yes! I will look for and find the positive in every situation. Greatness is within me even when it doesn't show to everyone else. I will reestablish that in my mind and dare my obstacles to prove me wrong. I will prove my point with passion, ambition, and refusal to back down. I will find a way to turn lemons into lemonade. I will take the stones thrown at me and build my empire. I will take the words used against me and remember them for my future testimony. I will take the lies and gossip spread about me; I will use them to teach people words will never define you if your actions are saying something else. I will see the positives in every negative. Curve ball or straight, I will swing, and I will hit many more times than I miss because I will adjust. I will increase my light as the world tries to increase its darkness. No matter how impossible the task may seem, I will find a way and an area of possibility to cling to.

CHAPTER 19

Success is not just my privilege, it is my responsibility.

No one likes a cheater. No one respects a cheater. Therefore, I will not cheat myself out of the success I'm pursuing by being lazy or submitting to destructive habits. I will not cheat myself out of abundance by thinking small or being afraid to fail. I owe myself the success I'm capable of, and I will not sell myself short. It is because of my potential that success is my responsibility, and I will not run from that responsibility.

CHAPTER 20

I don't do excuses.

I'm pretty sure someone would understand if I let my upbringing stop me. I know someone would empathize with the racism, sexism, ageism, or any other generalization I may have faced as I attempted to succeed. Heartbreak isn't a bad reason to quit. Abuse, addiction, and depression are all good reasons as well. Being raised by a single parent who works multiple jobs or seeing dysfunction my entire life so much it's normal; that would take the sting out of losing. However, I have no interest in excuses. I don't care who had everything handed to them and the fact I've had to scrape to survive and grind for everything I own. That doesn't matter to life, and it doesn't matter to me. I will explore another path, take another route, find directions, or whatever it takes in order to reach my destination. I simply do not do excuses. I do solutions.

CHAPTER 21

I will reach my dreams by any grind necessary.

Winning is my way of life because I'm willing to do what others won't. I'm willing to get up earlier, get my hands dirtier, and go harder than everyone else. I don't play to win. I play to dominate. I will stay humble, but I will work with a chip on my shoulder that it's humanly impossible to work harder than I do. I will not let my pride nor instant gratification get in the way of what I've set out to accomplish. I will grind to not only get it, but also keep it. No ethical or legal work it takes to win is beneath me. My grind is boundless and so will be the fruits of my labor.

CHAPTER 22

I will deliver for those depending on me.

I understand that those who love and know me the most want the best for me. I know my future children will look to me to be their provider, teacher, and support system. I know my family loves me and wants me to go as far as my gifts can take me. I understand that I'm a reflection of them everywhere I go, and it is for that reason that I can and will deliver. I will not let them down. I will exceed even their high expectations of me with the power of their love pushing me every step of the way. They saw greatness in me before I saw it in myself, but now that I can see it, I won't stop until it's blatantly obvious to the world.

CHAPTER 23

I accept being underrated.

I don't know if it'll be for a short while or a long period of time, but I accept being looked over. I embrace this time of not being on anyone's radar. I welcome the obscurity as I build in silence. I will not rush my process because there is no need to be impatient for what is sure to come. Without the applause or recognition, what I'm doing still holds significant value. I embody the humility needed to progress in privacy, and that's why I excel. I will not let my pride foolishly drive me to invest in premature attention that will cause me to act out of character. I will stay true to myself, and if the only way to do that is to be underrated, I'm just fine with that.

CHAPTER 24

I don't need their acceptance to accept myself.

I'm on a different path, so no, they shouldn't understand. I won't beg them or expect them to. I came into this world without their adoration, and I can live in this world just fine without it. I will view their lukewarm conversations, half-hearted smiles, and whispers behind my back as more reasons to appreciate my real family and friends. I will not beg anyone to realize that I'm amazing. I will not allow my evolution to be hindered by their small minds. I will continue to dream big.

CHAPTER 25

I have so much more to gain than I have to lose.

What's ahead of me is better than what's behind me. What I'm capable of getting right matters more than what I've already gotten wrong. My capabilities outmatch my shortcomings. I will focus on the fact that the opportunity to gain everything is more important than the risk of losing something. The world is vast, and so are my talents and creativity. Although I'm prone to focusing on small problems until they appear big, I will keep in mind that there is so much more going on in the world that I do not see that could be mine if I allowed myself to focus on it. My entire life can change forever and for the better in an instant, so I will not drown in the fear of what could go wrong. I will hold my head high and pointed towards my future instead of low so I can fear rock bottom.

CHAPTER 26

I will not feel guilty for cutting off cancerous friends.

My motivation is sacred. My drive is precious. I'm human, and don't always feel as capable as I am. Therefore, it's in my best interest to create distance between myself and those who don't have my best interests at heart. I am not wrong for it. I do not feel bad for it and rightfully so. Protecting my energy is a necessity and losing "friends" who are dead weights on this already treacherous journey is a sacrifice I'm willing to make. Those who will benefit in the future from the things I'm accomplishing now will thank me for it. I will thank myself for it once I realize the road I could have been taken down on. Any person who is not rowing on my boat is only causing it to sink and they have no right to be in it. My presence is a privilege that I've invested tremendously in to make it of value. I will not waste that value on anyone.

CHAPTER 27

I'm too valuable to allow myself to get lost in the pursuit of success.

I know this journey to a better life comes with its sacrifices, but I will not be one of them. Not my good heart. Not my kindness to and consideration of others. Not my morals that allow me to sleep peacefully at night. Not my family. These things, I will not part with in the pursuit of success, but I will, however, give up any part of me that is holding me back from my full potential. My immaturity. My laziness. My proneness to be distracted. My excuses. My small thinking. Being disorganized. These things that do not contribute to the best of me are not me. They are only dead skin that I will gladly shed as I grow into this new space in my life. Everything else will stay and I will have both the prosperity so many aim for as well as the core that makes it all worth it that so many lose along the way.

Chapter 28

Not quitting will pay off.

In the middle of the night when everyone else is asleep and no one sees me fighting my sleep to get just a little closer to my dreams, my goals are looking. When my head is pounding, but I refuse to stop until I've hit my daily objective I set for myself when I first woke up, my future is watching me. When I'm knee-deep in depression that no one else knows about, and the weight of the world is on my shoulders as I crawl a little further towards the finish line out of sheer determination, my purpose has its eye on me. When I feel helpless in my heartbreak, sickness, and loneliness, yet I continue to fight anyway, my endeavors are right there with me. The hard work I'm putting in may not be clear to others right now, but they are in no way being ignored. They are just preparing themselves for the grand entrance that happens only when I refuse to quit and make it to the end. That's the payout. I see it the entire time, everyone else sees it later when I tell them the story about everything they missed up until that point. I will get there when I've turned down the offer to quit enough times. Until then, I will continue to reject the proposition to do so for I know that every refusal is a step in the right direction.

CHAPTER 29

Money will not make me, but I will make plenty.

I desire riches, but my heart is not dictated by them. I want the best out of life, but I will not sell my soul for it. While I know that I can't take anything that I earn to the grave with me, I will still get plenty of it while I'm here. If I'm worth it, I want it all. God wants me to have it so long as I won't compromise my moral compass to obtain it. With that in mind, I will strive to make as much as I can and put it to the best use I can. I will be unselfish with my money and do for those who are trying, but can't do for themselves. It would be selfish of me to settle for less out of comfort, instead of striving to get the absolute most I can so I can use that to help others around me. I wouldn't be where I am today if everyone who helped me only had enough energy, time, and other resources for themselves. So I will strive more than I need for just myself and I will do good things with it for others.

CHAPTER 30

Everyone can't come.

There will be some changes that will hurt for a while, and they will come in the form of friends, real friends, who were simply not ready to grow with me. Life is going to charge me certain people that I thought would be around forever as I leave where I started and head towards the top, and I will pay that price. It won't be comfortable, and I may feel some guilt about doing it, but I must do it anyway and trust that their season may be gone but new seasons await me. I will continue building relationships that facilitate my growth, not stunt it. I will cherish the memories I've made with everyone, but I will not allow myself to be so stuck in the past that I don't go courageously towards my future. I will love them from the distance that allows me to evolve, the same way I would allow them to do if they were progressing at a different pace. I want the best for them, since they are my friends. I'm sure they want what's best for me even if it doesn't include them. I take comfort in that truth.

CHAPTER 31

Being broke will be a distant memory.

I have no moral obligation to financially struggle my entire life, so I won't. Paycheck to paycheck does not have to be my reality. Seeing people around me who need resources I don't have is not a sentence I will serve for starting with nothing. I reject those things and accept my ability to change them. I will be smarter in my finances and responsible in my spending. I will save more and invest better so that money does not come between anyone I love and the help they'll need. I deserve to enjoy great things, see many places, and do them with the mental freedom that my well-being is not in jeopardy. I will not be chained to a low standard of living because I can't do better, but only if it's the part of the process to doing better where I live below my means. I will not grow comfortable with my financial position of disparity because with all of the gifts I've been blessed with, prosperity is well within my grasp. I will one day see the days of me being broke as a distant memory, not an everyday reality.

THE END

Thank you for reading. If you enjoyed this, please let us and your friends know with an honest review or via any of my official social media handles listed below.

Facebook: https://www.facebook.com/officialderrickjaxn

Instagram: https://www.instagram.com/derrickjaxn

CPSIA information can be obtained
at www.ICGtesting.com
Printed in the USA
LVOW12s0719050917
547575LV00001B/3/P